How To Hear God
A 50-Day Devotional

CROSSING CHURCH
PUBLISHING
freegrace.tv
Guilt free. Grace full.

How To Hear God
A 50-Day Devotional

Copyright © 2016 The Crossing Church

Published by Crossing Church Publishing
829 School Street, Elk River, Minnesota 55330

Lead Pastors Eric & Kelly Dykstra. Edited by Tracy Keech.
Contributors: Silas Austin, Mike Curtis, Reuben Deisch, Braden Dykstra, Eric Dykstra, Kelly Dykstra, Nick Kantor, Jason Keech, Tracy Keech, Amy Kingore, Karli Phelps, Ben Saffrin, Alisia Sandstrom, Maria Sandstrom, Ted Snyder, Brian Sparks, Alisyn Studeman, Christy Turner, and Lynn Woolhouse.

www.freegrace.tv

All rights reserved. This book is protected by the copyright laws of the United States of America. This book may not be copied or reprinted for commercial gain or profit. The use of short quotations or occasional page copying for personal or group study is permitted and encouraged.

All scripture quotations, unless otherwise indicated, are taken from the Holy Bible, New International Version®, NIV®. Copyright ©1973, 1978, 1984, 2011 by Biblica, Inc.™ Used by permission of Zondervan. All rights reserved worldwide. www.zondervan.com The "NIV" and "New International Version" are trademarks registered in the United States Patent and Trademark Office by Biblica, Inc.™

Scripture quotations marked NKJV are taken from the NEW KING JAMES VERSION. Copyright © 1982 by Thomas Nelson, Inc. Used by permission. All rights reserved.

Scripture quotations marked NLT are taken from the *Holy Bible*, New Living Translation, copyright © 1996, 2004, 2007 by Tyndale House Foundation. Used by permission of Tyndale House Publishers, Inc., Carol Stream, Illinois 60188. All rights reserved.

Scripture quotations marked ESV are from The Holy Bible, English Standard Version® (ESV®), copyright © 2001 by Crossway, a publishing ministry of Good News Publishers. Used by permission. All rights reserved.

Scripture quotations marked MSG are taken from The Message. Copyright © 1993, 1994, 1995, 1996, 2000, 2001, 2002, 2003 by Eugene H. Peterson. Used by permission of NavPress Publishing Group.

First Printing: 2016

ISBN-13: 978-09896828-4-8 (Crossing Church Publishing)
ISBN-10: 0989682846

From Pastors Eric & Kelly

Congratulations on making an investment in your faith journey! Here's a quick note on what this book is about. It's designed to do a few things.

First, to give you a launching point for spending a few minutes focusing on the things of God and faith each day for 50 days.

Second, to explore the concepts of the spiritual disciplines. Meaning, elements and habits we can develop that will tend to position us to hear the voice of God and see Him at work in our lives.

Third, to spark conversation between you and others who are walking alongside you in faith, and to inspire you to share the hope of Jesus with someone new.

This book is not written by a panel of theological experts, rather, each day is straight from the heart and personal experience of a member of The Crossing Church staff. From office staff to technical assistant to finance director to campus pastors, each of us share candidly what we have learned on our faith journey.

Our prayer is that your journey will be enriched and that these 50 days will begin a lifetime of intentional time with your Heavenly Father, who is your never-ending source of grace and life.

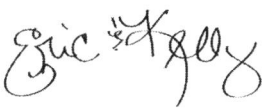

Don't we all want to know exactly what God is saying? This **How To Hear God 50-Day Devotional** is designed to help you focus on spiritual practices that help you connect with God every day for the next seven weeks (plus one bonus day!).

We believe that as you lean in and learn more about these spiritual disciplines, you will be able to hear God's voice more clearly.

Week 1
SAVIOR

Week 2
SCRIPTURE

Week 3
SABBATH REST

Week 4
SACRED FRIENDSHIPS

Week 5
SHARING YOUR HEART

Week 6
SILENCE & SOLITUDE

Week 7
SENT ONES

SAVIOR

From my heart to the Heavens,
Jesus be the center.
It's all about You.
Yes, it's all about You.

- Israel Houghton -

SAVIOR – Day 1

Scripture for Today:
Abide in Me, and I in you. As the branch cannot bear fruit of itself, unless it abides in the vine, neither can you, unless you abide in Me. I am the vine, you are the branches. He who abides in Me, and I in him, bears much fruit; for without Me you can do nothing.
(John 15:4-5 NLT)

Stay Connected To Christ
Things start to die when they get disconnected. A car will not start if you disconnect the battery cables. A branch withers up and dies if it gets disconnected from the trunk. A phone that does not eventually get plugged in is just an expensive paper weight. I think you get the idea. Things stall out, don't work, or die when they get disconnected from their source of power.

The same thing is true for you and me. If we get disconnected from Christ, we will stall out, become dysfunctional, or wither up spiritually. The key to being alive and fruitful is to stay connected to Christ. He is the source of power for our lives.

The verse we read today says something pretty extreme. It says, "apart from me you can do nothing." What if you took that to heart today? What if you actually believed you can do NOTHING without Christ? That without time in His Word, prayer, and worship, you cannot function properly.

And what if you believe the opposite of that truth as well? *Connected to Christ you can do anything!* All things are possible with a connection to Christ as your power source! So today, take time for prayer, read His word, worship Him as you drive to work, listen for His voice, and then, whatever He says, go out and do it! Your connection to Christ is your source of power!

What Does God Want For You Today?

_____
_____
_____
_____
_____
_____
_____
_____

A Prayer For Today:
Heavenly Father, I believe that only by staying close to You will I have the power to accomplish all things. Today I choose to walk with you, listen to Your voice, read Your word, and do Your will. Give me the power I need to do all the things You planned for me. May I be fruitful and alive today. In Jesus' name, Amen.

- Written by Eric Dykstra

SAVIOR – Day 2

Scripture for Today:
For everything comes from him and exists by his power and is intended for his glory. All glory to him forever! Amen. (Romans 11:36 NLT)

God Is Bigger
Have you ever found yourself really stressed or anxious about something in your life? Maybe it's a deadline at work or school. Maybe there's a hiccup in one of your relationships. Maybe you are scared to check the mail because you're afraid of what bills you might find.

No matter what you're worried about today, there is one prevailing truth: God is bigger. When we forget how big God is, and how in control He is, our problems seem HUGE. However, when we remember that God is big, our problems become small.

The verse for today is a great reminder for us of this truth. God made everything. By nature, a created thing cannot be more complex than its creator. If God created the world you live in, then He has power over any issues that you are facing. In fact, the verse says that everything exists by His power – this means that He is continually holding everything together! God is literally the *source* of everything, and at the *center* of everything.

Take 60 seconds today to stare at the sky. Seriously – carve out one minute for this simple activity. Use this time to remember that compared to God, our problems are very small. Everything is made by Him, and He is in ultimate control of everything. When you do this, you will find that an overwhelming peace will cover you.

What Does God Want For You Today?

_____
_____
_____
_____
_____
_____
_____
_____

A Prayer For Today:

Heavenly Father, I believe that you created everything. I believe that You created me. Because of that truth, I can rest in the fact that You are my source, and that You are empowering me to live a peaceful and powerful life. Today I ask You to be the center of my thoughts and actions. Guide my activities, my conversations, and my attitude – all for Your glory. In Jesus' name, Amen.

-Written by Ted Snyder

SAVIOR – Day 3

Scripture for Today:
For God is the one who provides seed for the farmer and then bread to eat. In the same way, he will provide and increase your resources and then produce a great harvest of generosity in you. Yes, you will be enriched in every way so that you can always be generous. And when we take your gifts to those who need them, they will thank God. (2 Corinthians 9:10-11 NLT)

God's Got It All
Close your eyes and imagine... Ok, don't close your eyes - just imagine you never having to wonder or worry about how you're going to be taken care of. Now stop imagining. Seriously, God's got it all. Everything everyone already has, God provided. When we pay that bill or swipe our card to buy our groceries, God paid for them.

From now on, whenever you give or pay a bill, just say to yourself, "God's got it all." You don't have to cross your fingers and toes every time you tithe or when you're generous to someone in need. God promises that He's got it all, and He's going to take care of you beyond what you can even imagine.

The verses we read today prove this point. "God is the one who provides seed." Not only does God provide the seed, it goes on to say that He will provide and increase your resources and then produce a great harvest of generosity in you. How amazing is that?! That verse gets better and better. God will provide, increase, and produce a great harvest for you to bless others. From there it gets even better. When we take our gifts to those in need, they will thank God. How easy is that? All we do is give those in need what has been given to us, and they will see God. No need for a soap box or waving a

"Jesus is Coming Back" sign in front of someone's face. Today you can fearlessly bless those in need with what God already provided for you.

What Does God Want For You Today?

_____
_____
_____
_____
_____
_____
_____
_____

A Prayer For Today:
Heavenly Father, thank you for providing everything I have. I ask for You to give me a name of someone to be generous to today, and pray that they'll see You in my generosity. Thank You for continuing to provide for me so I can be generous to others.
In Jesus' name, Amen.

-Written by Brian Sparks

SAVIOR – Day 4

Scripture For Today:
And my God will meet all your needs according to the riches of his glory in Christ Jesus. (Philippians 4:19 NIV)

Stress-Free God
We all have needs in life. We need food, water, clothing, and shelter to survive. Needs are important (that's why they're called "needs," we NEED them). But sometimes doesn't it seem like needs are hard to get? We work every day to achieve these needs, but sometimes they're still a huge stress to obtain.

I know I was stressed when my car got backed into in my driveway and I had to figure out how to pay to fix it. I know I was stressed when I had to pay for a new phone and also pay rent in the same week. I know I was stressed when I had to pay my college tuition. These things we need in life sometimes seem difficult to get.

But do you know what that verse just said? "And my God will meet ALL of your needs." I don't know about you, but "all" seems like ALL of my needs. That verse says that no matter what comes up against us, God will meet all of our needs. I don't need to stress about making my rent payment. All I have to do is keep working, and keep focusing on God. I will do my part, and I will let God do His.

Why would we ever need to stress if we knew that the God of the universe, the Guy that can take the world and stick it in His back pocket, is looking out for us? What if you lived with that kind of faith today? What if you decided to quit stressing and starting trusting God? I bet you would find peace, and I guarantee God will come through for you. Don't stress about being provided for, because God is NOT stressed.

What Does God Want For You Today?

_____
_____
_____
_____
_____
_____
_____
_____

A Prayer For Today:
God, thank You that You are our ultimate Provider. Thank You that You are not stressed, so neither am I. As I go though my day, help me to stay focused on You. Thank You that though life can surprise me, I can continue to rest, knowing that You are taking care of everything. Thank You, Jesus, for Your provision. In Jesus' name, Amen.

-Written by Braden Dykstra

SAVIOR – Day 5

Scripture for Today:
Do not conform to the pattern of this world, but be transformed by the renewing of your mind. Then you will be able to test and approve what God's will is – His good, pleasing and perfect will.
(Romans 12:2 NLT)

Start with Jesus
In our fast-paced world, it is so easy to get caught up in the daily grind and lose sight of our true purpose in life - to enjoy a Christ-centered life and allow His will to be active in our life.

We become so engrossed with the expectations of life (paying bills, tasks, etc.) we sometimes forget that God wants to make our life easier. He planned it all out. We just have to step into what He has for us and try not to allow the things of this world to consume our attention more than God.

Some people live from one awesome experience to the next, and their relationship with God is based on their feelings in the moment. They wonder why these experiences are so few and far between. How can we change that? As we consider this question, the place to start is with Jesus. A God-centered life will be a Christ-centered life, because Jesus Himself stands at the very center of our relationship with God

A Christ-centered life is shaped by two core principles: First, Jesus Christ is *alive*. As Christians, we do not follow a *dead* example, but a living Lord. God raised Jesus from the dead, and He sits (right now) at the throne of God. But Jesus does not simply sit around. Secondly, Jesus Christ is *working right now on our behalf!* So, when we invite Him into our day, and throughout our day, we are able to step into the fullness He already mapped out for us.

What Does God Want For You Today?

_____
_____
_____
_____
_____
_____
_____
_____

A Prayer For Today:
Heavenly Father, please allow me to function in this world, but not be affected by this world. Give me ears to hear what I need. Allow me to keep my focus on You alone. I believe that only by staying close to You will I have the power to accomplish all things. Thank You for Your enabling grace and extraordinary love. In Jesus' name, Amen.

-Written by Maria Sandstrom

SAVIOR – Day 6

Scripture for Today:
By Him all things hold together… (Colossians 1:16 NIV)

You Only Stay Together When You Stay Together
When I was a kid, my mom would drop my brother and me off at this little amusement park in Des Moines to ride the rides and enjoy ourselves for the day. When she dropped us off, she would always say the same thing. "Eric, Marc, you kids stay together!"

She wanted us to stay together because she knew that we would probably be better off if we did.

The same is true for us and Jesus. We need to STAY TOGETHER with Christ if want to be better off! The verse we read today is super important. It says that all things hold together by the power of Christ. The universe keeps going because Jesus holds it together. The sun keeps shining because Jesus holds it together. The earth keeps spinning because Jesus holds it together. But not just the big things… Your family stays together because Jesus holds it together. Your career keeps moving forward because Jesus holds it together. Your finances are the way they are because Jesus holds them together. Scripture says ALL THINGS are held together by Christ.

Here is why this matters to you today: If all things are held together by Christ, it is probably a pretty good idea for you to stay together with Christ. Don't wander off on your own today. Don't go making your own decisions and forgetting about the Savior. Walk with Christ today. Talk with Him. Invite Him into your day. Spend the day with Jesus like I used to spend the day at the amusement park with my brother. As we stick close to the One who is holding all things together, He will hold us together today.

What Does God Want For You Today?

_____
_____
_____
_____
_____
_____
_____
_____
_____

A Prayer For Today:
Heavenly Father, I believe You hold all things together through Your Son, Jesus. Today I invite Christ into my day. I ask Him to lead me and guide me. May I hear the voice of Christ and feel His presence as I work, rest, play, and live. May you hold my life together as I stay close to You. In Jesus' name, Amen.

-Written by Eric Dykstra

SAVIOR – Day 7

Scripture for Today:
Through him all things were made; Without him nothing was made that has been made. (John 1:3 NIV)

Without Him Nothing…
Ever think about how stuff is made? I do! I even love to watch shows about it. It fascinates me to figure out the processes and steps behind the finished products we see everyday! Maybe it's because I have a background in manufacturing.

I also love making stuff! There is something cool about taking raw materials and forming them into something amazing. I worked in manufacturing for years, and I loved working on processes to create something complete and finished. Recently, I made one of my favorite things - a fishing rod. It is so cool! Now don't get me wrong, it's not perfect, but I use it more than any other rod I have! It is a one-of-a-kind custom rod, made by me, for me, to do one thing: catch fish!!

That's why I love this verse in John 1. Without Him nothing was made. Without Him nothing… You were created for a purpose. Without Him, we are nothing. Without Him, there is nothing.

I know what you are thinking. "But I'm not perfect. I have flaws!" You know what? My fishing rod does, too. If you look real close, you will find little imperfections - little things that aren't just right. But, I still love it. I catch a ton of fish with it. It's my favorite. You are Jesus' favorite. He wants to live with you and in you. He wants to do amazing things with you! Will you let Him? Don't let a list of flaws keep you from doing amazing things. Jesus created you, He custom made you, and He loves you.

What Does God Want For You Today?

_____
_____
_____
_____
_____
_____
_____
_____

A Prayer for Today:
Heavenly Father, thank You for custom making me! I know You can use me, even with my flaws. Thank You for loving me. Thank You for giving me a purpose! Use my life to do amazing things. I know if I am in your hands, good things will happen. Without You, nothing. I am everything in Your hands! I am all Yours. In Jesus' name, Amen.

-Written by Jason Keech

SCRIPTURE

**The more you read the Bible,
The more you'll love its Author.**

- Unknown -

SCRIPTURE – Day 1

Scripture for today:
With my whole heart I seek you; let me not wander from your commandments! I have stored up your word in my heart, that I might not sin against you.
(Psalm 119:10-11 ESV)

Packed And Ready
If you are a parent, you understand what it's like to pack a diaper bag so you'll be prepared for ANYTHING to happen!

Your kid wants a snack? You packed one. Your son blows out his diaper? You brought more! Your daughter lost her Elsa doll at some point during the day? You were smart and packed an extra Elsa doll. As a parent, you become good at thinking this way.

As followers of Christ who seek Him with their whole heart, this is the mentality we need to have as well. That verse uses the words, "I have stored up your word in my heart." This means you have stored up scripture in your head and in your heart so that when you walk into a tough time in life, you have the living and active words of God readily accessible to guide you through any and every situation.

How different would your day be if you had God's Word stored up in your heart? What if you were always loaded with scripture to bring you faithfully through the tough times?

I'm challenging you, find a verse for the week, memorize it word for word, and then next week pick a different one. Build up your library of memorized Bible verses so you can be packed and ready for the unexpected turns of life.

What Does God Want For You Today?

_____
_____
_____
_____
_____
_____
_____
_____

A Prayer For Today:
Jesus, I believe that Your Word is alive and active and is able to impact the deepest parts of my soul. Today and this week as I seek you with everything I have by storing up Your Word in my heart, I pray that I would look more like You, think more like You, and act more like You – simply because I am investing in the words You spoke. I thank You and praise You! In Jesus' name, Amen.

-Written by Ben Saffrin

SCRIPTURE – Day 2

Scripture for Today:
My child, listen to what I say, and treasure my commands. Tune your ears to wisdom, and concentrate on understanding. Cry out for insight, and ask for understanding. Search for them as you would for silver; seek them like hidden treasures. Then you will understand what it means to fear the Lord, and you will gain knowledge of God. For the Lord grants wisdom! (Proverbs 2:1-6 NLT)

The Answer Key
How did you prepare for your last test? Did you spend weeks, days, hours, or minutes studying? Or worse, did you "cram"? How much of that knowledge did you retain? Life is a test, and the Bible is your study guide.

When you study little by little, day by day, you retain knowledge better, and probably score better on a test. Don't you want the same for this test of life? God provides the answers and tools for this life on earth through His Word. You can pass because He has already given you the answer key!

God did not intend for the study of His Word to be overwhelming, boring, or something to be put off until crunch time. Studying the Bible is how our Creator connects with us as we read, pray, and spend time in His presence.

Sometimes we feel rushed, agitated, or overwhelmed with life, so we skip out on spending time with God. But these are the times it is most important to dive into the Bible! No matter what you're going through, pause and ask God for the desire to spend time with Him in His Word. There you will find the answers you need during a struggle. Pass this test and be an A student daily!

What Does God Want For You Today?

_____
_____
_____
_____
_____
_____
_____
_____

A Prayer For Today:

Heavenly Father, open my mind, heart, and soul for what You want to teach me through Your Word. May the time I spend studying the Bible give me clarity, peace, and wisdom for the tests of life I face today. In Jesus' name, Amen.

-Written by Lynn Woolhouse

SCRIPTURE – Day 3

Scripture for Today:
Keep this Book of the Law always on your lips; meditate on it day and night. (Joshua 1:8 NIV)

Studying Your Bible
What do you think of when you hear the word "study?" If you're like me, you have some negative experiences related to that word. When I think of study, I recall the many hours of "required" reading of boring textbooks in college. This is NOT the type of study we are talking about...and if you're in school, don't let one boring textbook steal your passion for learning about the things God has designed you to enjoy! Finishing that boring textbook could get you a job some day.

Did you know that the word "study" is actually rarely used in the Bible? In fact, the Bible in one place says to be careful NOT to study too much (Ecclesiastes 12:12)! Very often, the scripture uses the word "meditate." To meditate means to ponder something, or to murmur out loud or in your head!

Has anyone ever caught you talking to yourself? ...guess what, congratulations, you were MEDITATING. You already are a man or woman of God! Over and over again, scripture teaches us to meditate on God's word (Psalm 77:12; Psalm 143:5). God's heart is that we would KNOW Him and love Him the same way we know our best friend or a spouse!

One of the simplest ways to get to know God is to read His Word. But relax, this doesn't need to be stressful! It's not about an intellectual pursuit. God's desire is that we spend time getting to know Him, and then we take time to ponder what He is doing and what He has done in our life! Scripture says that Jesus Himself would often go alone by Himself to ponder with God (Mark 1:35). Do you have enough quiet moments in your life to meditate on God's Word? Maybe it's early in the morning, late at night, or on your car ride to work. Find a moment today to read scripture and enjoy a moment of meditation.

What Does God Want For You Today?

_____
_____
_____
_____
_____
_____
_____
_____

A Prayer For Today:
Heavenly Father, I ask that You would rekindle a passion to know You! Place in me a desire and a hunger to understand Your Word. Cause it to come alive in my heart. Let me experience the joy and mystery of knowing You. Help me to enjoy my time with You, exactly the way You have designed me to enjoy it. In Jesus' name, Amen.

-Written by Nick Kantor

SCRIPTURE – Day 4

Scripture for Today:
For the word of God is alive and powerful...
(Hebrews 4:12a NLT)

Alive and Powerful
Think about the person you would consider your "hero" – the person you look up to the most and want to be like. If that person wrote you a letter, what would you do? Would you put it on a shelf and look at it occasionally out of guilt, or would you read it over and over again because you want to commit those words to heart?

That's what the Bible is! Your Creator put His words for you into a Book so that you can hear what He has to say every day of your life. He's got a little bit of everything in there: poetry, history, adventure, life coaching, counseling, encouragement... all working together to tell the best news you'll ever hear.

The thing about the Bible is that it's not a typical book. The verse we read today says that the Word of God is ALIVE and POWERFUL. That means that it's impossible to read it and stay the same. You can't read it and not experience life change. God's Word brings wisdom, hope, healing, justice, forgiveness... the list is endless. The Bible is a treasure trove, and diving into what God says will always leave you a different person.

There are hundreds of tools you can use to begin your journey into the Word of God. Find what works for you and do it! You'll be amazed at what God will do as you begin to explore and study and learn.

Don't ignore the letter that God wrote to you; invest in His Word, and watch YOURSELF become more alive and powerful as it changes you for the better.

What Does God Want For You Today?

_____
_____
_____
_____
_____
_____
_____
_____

A Prayer For Today:
God, thank You for Your Word and how You are continually growing and changing me when I read it. I choose to value the words You've written for me by investing my time in studying them and meditating on them. Help me to find a groove for studying Your Word so that it becomes a habit in my life. In Jesus' name, Amen.

-Written by Karli Phelps

SCRIPTURE – Day 5

Scripture for Today:
These were more fair-minded than those in Thessalonica, in that they received the word with all readiness, and searched the Scriptures daily to find out whether these things were so.
(Acts 17:11 NKJV)

Scripture is our Fact Checker
As Christians, we are called to be disciples and to make disciples. We are called to continue to search God and grow in wisdom and stature and favor with God and man, just like Jesus. Searching and studying scripture is how Jesus did this, and it is how we can do it as well.

As new believers, many times, we are ready and eager to hear more from people who we believe know more than we do about God's grace and truth. We listen and soak up all we can from them. This is a good thing, but we need to remember to always go back to scripture to see if what they said in fact lines up with what the Word says.

When we study scripture and know it, we will recognize more quickly if someone or something is trying to lead us astray. We have a foundation of truth to stand on and build from. Scripture is truth, and that's the fact, Jack!

Then when we go out and share our faith and we know the scriptures, we can speak with authority. We speak not from our wisdom, but from the wisdom of God. This is another way that God never leaves you, because His truths are rooted in your heart and mind.

What Does God Want For You Today?

_____
_____
_____
_____
_____
_____
_____
_____

A Prayer For Today:
Heavenly Father, guide me by Your Word. I want to know You more, and so I ask that my appetite for Your truth is new every day. Give me a desire to be fed from Your Word each day so that I may grow into all You have created me for. In Jesus' name, Amen.

-Written by Silas Austin

SCRIPTURE – Day 6

Scripture for Today:
For the word of God is alive and powerful. It is sharper than the sharpest two-edged sword, cutting between soul and spirit, between joint and marrow. It exposes our innermost thoughts and desires. (Hebrews 4:12 NLT)

This Might Hurt A Little
God's Word is alive and powerful. I think most of us would agree. There are a lot of days when I read the Bible, and wow, it is so good!! I read a verse and it is exactly what I needed to hear! I walk away and it is "Happy Town" for me all day.

And it is good that His Word does that, right? I mean, it's just supposed to make us feel good so we can have a "peachy" day. But then I think, as a parent, my words for my kids aren't always received like that. Sometimes there is pushback. We as parents sometimes say things that our kids don't want to hear! "Clean your room." "Do the dishes." "Be polite." "Shake hands when you meet someone." "Do a job until it's done the right way." (Insert eye roll here, right?)

Have you ever had an eye roll moment while reading your Bible? Ever had a knot in the pit of your stomach moment while diving into His Word? You read that verse and it hits you in a way you don't like? It's true, God's Word is going to have it's moments when it makes us feel good, but there are also going to be moments when our Heavenly Daddy needs us to do things we may not want to do.

I think those are the cutting moments. The moments when His Word hurts a little. Let it happen! Lean into it. Allow our Heavenly Daddy to perform surgery on you and change you into a better person. Maybe God is trying to do something good with those verses. Would you let Him speak to you? Allow God to speak into your life. Today, really listen to Him, even if it's something difficult to hear, walk away changed and healed in the process!

What Does God Want For You Today?

_____
_____
_____
_____
_____
_____
_____
_____

A Prayer For Today:
Heavenly Father, I know there are times when I want to blow off your Word. There are times when I want to be told I'm great, and not hear the hard things that are in my heart. May I lean in to whatever You want to say, and then be changed to be more like You! In Jesus' name, Amen.

-Written by Jason Keech

SCRIPTURE – Day 7

Scripture for Today:
...we take captive every thought to make it obedient to Christ. (2 Corinthians 10:5 NLT)

Maybe It's Time
Have you ever had a terrible roommate? They invade your privacy and always pay rent late. They eat all your food and invite the irritating neighbor over to play Rock Band until the wee hours of the morning. The last time they took out the trash or washed the dishes Nirvana was the hot new band. Life becomes miserable and chaotic and tiring because we are constantly annoyed in a place that is supposed to be our safe haven from the worries of the world – our home.

Our brain is where all our thoughts live. Some thoughts are great ideas, some make you smile, and some are like that terrible roommate. They just need to go, because they're robbing you of the ability to be at peace.

Maybe it's time to evict those thoughts that live in your head. You know the ones. "I'm not good enough." "I'll never be able to." "They don't like me." "Nobody else will ever understand." "God will never forgive me for that."

One of the key ways to find out if we should kick a thought to the curb is to see if it lines up with what the Bible says. If it doesn't, it has to go. But we can only know if it lines up with God's truth if we are filling our minds up with scripture. This way, we're able to slam the door on the unruly thought before it has a chance to move grandma's old flowery couch into our living room.

What thoughts are keeping you from walking in the new life Christ gave you? Does it line up with the Word? Maybe it's time to give that thought its walking papers.

What Does God Want For You Today?

_____
_____
_____
_____
_____
_____
_____
_____

A Prayer For Today:
Heavenly Father, thank You for Your Word. Thank You for giving me discernment and making me more wise as I spend time with You reading scripture. Will you help me identify which thoughts line up with the Your truth and which need to be kicked out? I am grateful that You want me to thrive! In Jesus' name, Amen.

-Written by Tracy Keech

SABBATH REST

Without worship, we go about miserable.

- A.W. Tozer -

SABBATH REST – Day 1

Scripture for Today
Keep the Sabbath day holy. Don't pursue your own interest on that day, but enjoy the Sabbath and speak of it with delight as the Lord's holy day. Honor the Sabbath in everything that you do on that day, and don't follow your own desires or talk idly. (Isaiah 58:13 NLT)

Resting in God
I love this verse! It's a good reminder that the Sabbath was created for me! It's a gift from God! This verse says that the Sabbath wasn't created just for us to observe, but to enjoy. I like that!

Life gets busy, and it doesn't seem to be slowing down anytime soon. It's so easy to get caught up in everything the world has to offer. Work, school, sports, kids, chores, and even serving at church or a local non-profit…these things are good! However, if we fill our week with too much stuff, we forget to leave room for God.

I think it's easy to fall into one of two categories. We either get too busy to take time off to enjoy the Sabbath, or we make the Sabbath all about us and leave God out. It's not just about us - it's about us connecting with God, giving Him thanks for everything. The Sabbath isn't just about rest, it's about worship. It's about honor. Do what you enjoy, but put God in the center.

The Sabbath wasn't created to make us feel guilty for saying yes to too many things. It was created so that we can live guilt free when we say no to some things, and so that we can give Him thanks.

What Does God Want For You Today?

_____
_____
_____
_____
_____
_____
_____
_____

A Prayer For Today:
Heavenly Father, You have gifted me with a day of rest, a day to connect with You. I pray that I will see the importance in that. I pray that the busyness of the world doesn't keep me from spending time with You every week. Help me to reconnect with You. Prepare my heart and mind to rest in You, knowing that everything is in Your control. In Jesus' name, Amen.

-Written by Mike Curtis

SABBATH REST – Day 2

Scripture for Today:
By the seventh day God had finished his work. On the seventh day he rested from all his work. God blessed the seventh day. He made it a Holy Day because on that day he rested from his work, all the creating God had done... (Genesis 2:2-4 MSG)

No Rest For The Wicked
No rest for the wicked. We've all heard this phrase before. But it's more like "no rest makes us wicked." If you've ever stayed up for more than 24 hours, you know this is true. When you lack sleep, everyone who is around you knows it to be true, too. Your attitude starts to change and you get crabby. Any little thing can set you off into a Hulk-like rage. The same is true if you are working non-stop. This doesn't just mean working at your job non-stop; this includes activities you do outside of that. If you're constantly on the run and never stopping to take a day to rest, it becomes easier and easier to put God on the back burner.

A day of rest is really vital to not only a healthy physical life, but your spiritual life as well. If we are constantly on-the-go, at the end of every day our body is too exhausted to stop and think about how good God is and everything He did for us that day. Our only thought is getting to bed quickly because tomorrow is going to be just as busy as today. Before you know it, you miss church one week. After that, it gets a little easier to miss. Before long you get so burnt out, you can hardly function and bitterness sets in.

God is so powerful. He created everything with just His words. Do you really think He needed a break? Was He so tired from speaking He needed a nap? Of course not. But God knows that rest is important. It is so important that He made that seventh day a Holy Day. God is our example. As Christians we need to follow His example and take a rest. The Sabbath is a Holy Day to worship God for all He has done in our lives. You are like a battery. Each day your spiritual battery drains - its charge will only last six days. On that seventh day, you need to plug yourself in. When you plug your phone charger in to wall socket, it's best to keep it there until it's charged to 100%. Recharge yourself to 100% by taking that Holy Day of Sabbath rest.

What Does God Want For You Today?

_____
_____
_____
_____
_____
_____
_____
_____

A Prayer For Today:
Heavenly Father, thank You for being my example and for giving me a Sabbath. Today I choose to take a day once a week to rest and worship You. I believe that You will help take care of all the work that needs to get done so that I can rest. In Jesus' name, Amen.

-Written by Brian Sparks

SABBATH REST – Day 3

Today's Scripture
"Cease striving and know that I am God; I will be exalted among the nations, I will be exalted in the earth." (Psalms 46:10 NASB)

Rest Done Right IS Worship
Do you ever feel like if you stop for even a second your world could fall apart? Like you're too busy to even breathe? Does it seem that the weight of the world is on your shoulders and if you set it down you'll never be able to pick it up? That is not God's plan for you.

In this verse, God tells us to do the very thing that we feel we can't do. God says, "Cease striving." Most other translations say, "Be still," but this version lays it out directly. STOP TRYING SO HARD! God also tells us why it's ok to rest. He says, "…and know that I am God." God is telling us that He has it covered. He's not worried, and we don't need to be either.

The verse goes on to say that God will be exalted among the nations and in the world. In other words, God will be praised or worshipped everywhere. When we get to the point where we trust God enough to take a break; that's worship. Resting in God's completed work shows that we exalt Him and aren't relying on our own efforts.

What if we change our perspective of rest today? What if we look at it not as unproductive time, but instead as a time to show God we believe that He is in control. Let's use rest as a way to honor God. Jesus said that He wants to give us rest. Let's seek Jesus for rest, putting our trust in Him to carry us through.

What Does God Want For You Today?

_____
_____
_____
_____
_____
_____
_____
_____
_____

A Prayer For Today:
Heavenly Father, I know that You want me to put my trust in You in all things. Today I choose to come to You for rest. I believe that You can do more in my life while I honor You than I can do on my own. I ask that You restore my heart, mind, and strength today as I focus on You, knowing that You are always scheming behind the scenes to bless me. In Jesus' name, Amen.

-Written by Silas Austin

SABBATH REST – Day 4

Scripture for Today:
...in six days the Lord made heaven and earth, and on the seventh day He rested and was refreshed. (Exodus 31:17 NIV)

Supernatural Rest
Do you ever feel like you're just running through life with no moment to catch your breath? Do you work yourself into such a tire that you physically crash? Do you feel so fried that you lash out at those around you? Do you keep telling yourself, "If I can just finish this one thing, I can relax!"? Do you hate sitting still, and have a compulsion to fill every moment of your day with something to do? Do you feel like if you ever stop running, that everything will fall apart?

I have something to tell you: God rested! Let that sink in. The Creator of the entire Universe - past, present, and future - rested. When Jesus came to earth, He rested, knowing full well that His days on earth were limited. Jesus spent a short 33 years on this earth. In that time He had to lead disciples, heal the sick, mend broken hearts, cast out demons, and lay the groundwork for a movement which would still be around thousands of years later (the Church). Talk about not enough time in the day! If all that wasn't enough, He also died to save the ETERNITIES of people in the present and the future. The Son of God came to earth with all those responsibilities in mind, and yet He rested.

Jesus did this because He wants to set an example for us. God wants us to rest and feel refreshed in His presence. Imagine how much lighter your burdens would feel if you had a whole day where you did nothing but spend time with God! By saying no to errands and tasks one day a week, you now have time to say yes to Jesus!

He will give you the rest and refreshment you need to handle the six other days of the week! Think of it this way: if Jesus was physically in front of you and asked to spend one day with you, would you turn Him down to go run errands? Jesus may not physically be in front of you, but He is present and He is asking for your time!

What Does God Want For You Today?

_____
_____
_____
_____
_____
_____
_____
_____

A Prayer For Today:
Heavenly Father, thank You that You are a God that cares so much about my well-being! I pray that You give me the supernatural discipline to set one day aside for praising You. Holy Spirit, I pray that You open my heart to receive the supernatural rest and refreshment You have in store for me! I am so blessed that I get to spend time in Your presence! Thank You for dying so that I can also spend eternity with You! In Jesus' name, Amen.

-Written by Alisia Sandstrom

SABBATH REST – Day 5

Scripture for Today:
Then Jesus said to them, "The Sabbath was made to meet the needs of people, and not people to meet the requirements of the Sabbath." (Mark 2:27 NLT)

Sabbath: Rest and Worship
When you hear the word "Sabbath," what is the first thing that comes to mind? For some of you, you have pleasant thoughts about that one day where you finally get to relax. For others of you, you think of that one day that you "should" take off, but it never really works out… and then you kind of feel bad about it. If you're in the latter group, take heart, I've been there.

First of all, when you hear that word Sabbath, it just means taking a day off every week to rest and enjoy yourself! I used to view the Sabbath as an obligation, which meant I rarely enjoyed it and often thought about all the lost time I just gave up. That is not what God had in mind. After all, Jesus said it was not about "the REQUIREMENTS of the Sabbath."

A Sabbath day is about two things: resting and worship… and I'm NOT talking about sitting in your room and singing hymns for a day (Thank You, Jesus). God told His people to take a Sabbath because He knew that people get stressed! He knew that it would be good for everyone to take a break and relax… and He knew people probably wouldn't do it unless He told them: Everybody just RELAX (Ex. 23:12; that's my paraphrase). In fact, modern researchers have found that taking a break makes you MORE productive at work. And that's not cutting-edge research; God had the idea a few thousand years ago.

Secondly, the Sabbath is an act of worship. Meaning

this, taking a day off once a week tells God that we trust Him with our time! Our human instinct is to think, "I can't take a day off, I'll get behind!" I believe Jesus taught us to take a Sabbath because it's good for us… but I also believe it is an act of faith to trust God with our time. After all, in America your schedule can own you, or you can own your schedule. I want to encourage you with this today: if you need to take a break, find a way to take a break on a regular basis. I bet you will find yourself enjoying life more, trusting God more, and ready to work again.

What Does God Want For You Today?

_____
_____
_____
_____
_____
_____
_____
_____

A Prayer For Today:
Heavenly Father, I believe You know what's best for me. You know that I need rest and time to just enjoy life. Give me the faith to trust You with my time and energy. I ask You to show me what that could look like in my life, and I ask that You would give me the courage to take those steps. In Jesus' name, Amen.

-Written by Nick Kantor

SABBATH REST – Day 6

Scripture for Today:
Then Jesus said, "Come to me, all of you who are weary and carry heavy burdens, and I will give you rest. Take my yoke upon you. Let me teach you, because I am humble and gentle at heart, and you will find rest for your souls. For my yoke is easy to bear, and the burden I give you is light." (Matthew 11:28-30 NLT)

You are not being lazy; it's called a Sabbath
Have you ever stopped and thought, "I need a nap."? Have you ever woken up for work and thought, "I can't wait to get home tonight to relax!"? Now, how many times have you told yourself, "You can't nap! There's so much to get done!" Or how about, "If you do that, you're only being lazy!" Or the best, "I'll sleep when I'm dead."

Did you know that naps and relaxation are biblical? God referred to it as a day of rest or Sabbath. The Sabbath was intended as a day for you to spend with Him. As you rest, reflect on all He has done and provided for you over the last six days.

A Sabbath is, most importantly, a day with no work. (This includes, but is not limited to, e-mails; phone calls, or anything work-related. Send it to voicemail.) A Sabbath also includes reading scripture. God is the One who created the Sabbath, and He asks us to keep it holy. Dig into the scriptures and relax at home, and don't be afraid to treat yourself. This day of rest is meant to refresh you, so whether it's a long nap, good movie, a massage, a day on the boat, exercise, concert, whatever revitalizes you, do it! God says so.

The next time you call yourself lazy for taking a day to rest, know your Heavenly Father gave you that time to rejuvenate yourself for Him. You are not only refreshing his temple (your body), but you are worshiping your Creator by reflecting on the things He has given you as you spend time in the care, comfort, and relaxation of His presence and the life He has given you.

What Does God Want For You Today?

_____
_____
_____
_____
_____
_____
_____
_____

A Prayer For Today:
Heavenly Father, You are the Creator of the Universe and you also are the Creator of rest, and for that, I thank You so much. I ask today for You to help me understand and embrace the importance of setting aside a day just for You. I invite You into my Sabbath, and pray You will use this day to teach me to trust You and embrace Your presence. In Jesus' name, Amen.

-Written by Lynn Woolhouse

SABBATH REST – Day 7

Scripture For Today:
Remember to observe the Sabbath day by keeping it holy. You have six days each week for your ordinary work, but the seventh day is a Sabbath day of rest dedicated to the Lord your God... (Exodus 20:8-10 NLT)

Sabbath: The Great Stress-Killer
Stress is all in your mind. Yeah, I know it comes from an abundance of responsibilities or issues to deal with, but the difference between simply feeling the weight of life and feeling stressed out is found in the way you *think*.

This is what I love about a weekly Sabbath rest. It is a day set aside from your "ordinary work" and dedicated to receiving rest and refreshment that comes as a gift from God. You might think, *how does stopping work for a day ease stress? It's all waiting for me when I start working again!*

Well, let's go back to the part about stress being in your mind. If you BELIEVE that you are fully responsible for accomplishing all the "stuff" of your life, you will FEEL stress.

However, if you BELIEVE that God is fully responsible for accomplishing all your work, and you're simply a tool in His hand, you will FEEL calm.

The way you demonstrate that belief is by obeying God's plan for a healthy lifestyle: dedicate to Him a day of rest. When you honor God (and His design for your body and mind), you show that you trust Him to help you get your work done in the time He allotted for it.

Believe He is willing and able to accomplish everything you need to handle. Demonstrate that belief by honoring

His gift of a day of rest.

Work the other six days with the confidence that comes from knowing you're relying on Him; not you.

What Does God Want For You Today?

_____
_____
_____
_____
_____
_____
_____
_____

A Prayer For Today:
Heavenly Father, I don't like stress to rule my life. I am choosing to trust You to accomplish all I need to this week. I'm demonstrating that trust by setting aside time to receive Your rest and refreshment. Let me think and live from that place of rest and not from a place of stress. Thank You for designing such a beautiful plan for my physical and mental health. In Jesus' name, Amen.

-Written by Kelly Dysktra

SACRED FRIENDSHIPS

**What is a friend?
A single soul dwelling in two bodies.**

- Augustine -

SACRED FRIENDSHIPS – Day 1

Scripture for today:
...*The soul of Jonathan was knit to the soul of David, and Jonathan loved him as his own soul.*
(1 Samuel 18:1 ESV)

Everyone Needs a Jonathan
As you read the story of David, you watch as he goes through struggle after struggle, opposition after opposition, and fight after fight. But one of the amazing traits of David is his relentless faith. Time and time again he is faithful to be the man God called him to be and doesn't allow the forces against him to sway his faith. I think a big part of this is due to the people with whom he surrounded himself.

Jonathan, the prince of Israel and son of King Saul, time and time again encourages David and keeps him out of risky situations. Jonathan wasn't afraid to risk his reputation or even his life to protect David.

This is why having strong relationships and community with other like-minded believers is so important. The right people will bring you to the right places and cause you to do the right things.

Do you have any Jonathans in your life? Do you have people who keep you away from dangerous situations and remind you of all the good God has for you? Build relationships with people like Jonathan and watch how something as simple as having a good and loyal friend can totally change the direction of your life.

What Does God Want For You Today?

_____
_____
_____
_____
_____
_____
_____
_____

A Prayer For Today:
Jesus, I pray that You would help me build strong and healthy relationships in my life. Help me find loyal, honest, and Christ-like friends who will lead me closer to You. Give me the wisdom I need to give influence to the right people in my life. In Jesus' name, Amen.

-Written by Ben Saffrin

SACRED FRIENDSHIPS – Day 2

Scripture For Today:
Since God chose you to be the holy people he loves, you must clothe yourselves with tenderhearted mercy, kindness, humility, gentleness, and patience. Make allowance for each other's faults, and forgive anyone who offends you. Remember, the Lord forgave you, so you must forgive others. Above all, clothe yourselves with love, which binds us all together in perfect harmony. (Colossians 3:12-14 NLT)

Christ-Like Companionship
When I read this verse, I started to think about what it means to clothe myself in mercy, kindness, humility, gentleness, patience, and above all else - love. If we are not clothed in love, we are like a naked savage running around with spear in hand, ready to kill or be killed. I think that's what the world wants us to look like, to believe that, in the end, it is every man for himself.

The good news is that Jesus made us holy - set apart. God chose us as the holy people He loves. We were naked in the wilderness, and He gave us these clothes so that the world would know that our God is a good Heavenly Father.

By clothing ourselves in mercy, kindness, humility, gentleness, patience, and love, we are wearing the robes of royalty that were given to us by Jesus. Being clothed in these things brings blessings, not only to ourselves through supernatural peace, but to those around us. When we wear these things, people recognize that we are followers of Jesus Christ.

What Does God Want For You Today?

_____
_____
_____
_____
_____
_____
_____
_____
_____

A Prayer For Today:
Heavenly Father, I thank You that I do not have to live in this world doing life alone. I thank You that You love me enough to not only be with me in Spirit, but to give me earthly friendships that bring me closer to You! I pray that You give me the ability to see the daily opportunities I have to clothe myself in these things that bind us together in perfect harmony. I pray that my bold tenderheartedness shows those around me who You are, and how much you love us! I pray that in these things I can find the perfect peace that only comes from You! In Jesus' name, Amen!

-Written by Alisia Sandstrom

SACRED FRIENDSHIPS – Day 3

Scripture for Today:
Always be humble and gentle. Be patient with each other, making allowance for each other's faults because of your love. Make every effort to keep yourselves united in the Spirit, binding yourselves together with peace. (Ephesians 4:2-3 NLT)

By Our Love
When I was a kid, there was this song we used to sing in Sunday School: "They will know we are Christians by our love, by our love. They will know we are Christians by our love." Just as it is with our biological siblings, we won't always see eye-to-eye with our brothers and sisters in Christ. We may disagree about which music we want to sing in church or the best plan of action for inviting someone new to join our volunteer team. We may even disagree about some theological ideas.

People aren't perfect. Remembering to see all people as God sees them is a good way to exercise patience, peace, and gentleness, even when we disagree. When we focus on the fact that we are all united in the Spirit – that Jesus died for each one of us – we can stand together in unity and advance His message of hope.

A healthy community isn't one where everyone always gets along. It is one where grace is given, despite the faults, mistakes, or flaws of each individual. A healthy community is created when we operate as if everyone's welcome, nobody's perfect, and anything is possible.

Today, make a choice to be patient with each other. Make every effort to live in unity with the family of God. It is His peace that binds us all together. Is this always easy? No. But it sets an example for the rest of the world to know the love of Jesus.

What Does God Want For You Today?

_____
_____
_____
_____
_____
_____
_____
_____
_____

A Prayer For Today:
Heavenly Father, I believe that You want Christians to be known for our love for one another and the rest of the world. Thank You for seeing me with love, despite my flaws. Please help me to see others like you see me! Bring Your people together in unity so that Your love shines bright in our dark world. In Jesus' name, Amen.

-Written by Tracy Keech

SACRED FRIENDSHIPS – Day 4

Scripture for Today:
Just as our bodies have many parts and each part has a special function, so it is with Christ's body. We are all parts of His one body, and each of us has a different work to do. And since we are all one body in Christ, we belong to each other, and each of us needs all the others. (Romans 12: 4-5 NLT)

Together = Unstoppable
"No man is an island unto himself." My dad used to always say this to us boys growing up. I believe this holds true for the body of Christ, too! There are many of us, and we all perform different functions in the Church.

The ear cannot say to the nose, "I don't need you," and the nose cannot say to the ear, "I don't need you." Although they are both unique and function differently, they're both vital to a fully functional body.

What keeps us united as one is the love we have for Christ. When we all focus our attention on Christ and come together as one, we are all in harmony as a single body. It takes each individual in the church playing his or her role to accomplish the complete work of the body of Christ.

You matter. Your skills and gifts are necessary to the Body of Christ. We were all created to live in harmony, one with another. Christ has given us special talents and gifts. When we all put those to use for the glory of Him and the Church, as a whole we can be an unstoppable force for the Kingdom of God.

What Does God Want For You Today?

_____
_____
_____
_____
_____
_____
_____
_____

A Prayer for Today:

Dear Jesus, though we all perform different tasks and jobs, may we all be unified as one. May our love for You unite us as one, and may we all function in one accord, connected to You. In Jesus' name, Amen.

-Written by Reuben Deisch

SACRED FRIENDSHIPS – Day 5

Scripture for Today:
Don't just pretend to love others. Really love them. Hate what is wrong. Hold tightly to what is good. Love each other with genuine affection, and take delight in honoring each other. Never be lazy, but work hard and serve the Lord enthusiastically. (Romans 12:9-13 NLT)

Make Some New Friends
In life, we go through many seasons alone. The funny thing is, God did not intend for us to do life alone. He wants us to build relationships with others, and yes, this includes those "sinners" outside the church walls.

God called us all to be His hands and feet, to share the Good News. How can we do that if we seclude ourselves within the church walls, surrounded by only other believers? Maybe the idea of sharing Jesus with a stranger scares the daylights out of you. That's ok!

Here's a secret: being a part of a community outside of church is an easy way to build the relationships God called us to build. Here's why: to share Jesus with an unbeliever!

The next time you hesitate to make conversation with the chatty stranger at Target or decline an invite to your neighbor's BBQ, reconsider. You can love them like Jesus! Jesus' social circle didn't exclude thieves, tax collectors, or prostitutes, so why should yours exclude the needy neighbor or the friendly (yet a bit annoying) know-it-all at Home Depot?

Building relationships within your community gives you the perfect opportunity to share the Jesus in you. Not only will the people around you be infected (in a good way) by the love you share, but you will see the blessings Jesus has for you as you get out there!

These relationships will bring Him closer to each person you meet and show His love. So go make some new friends!

What Does God Want For You Today?

_____
_____
_____
_____
_____
_____
_____
_____
_____

A Prayer for Today:
Heavenly Father, thank You for sharing Your love with us each day through other people. Today I pray for You to give me the courage and the heart of Jesus to embrace relationships outside church walls. Give me the understanding, compassion, and desire to love like You. Provide me with opportunities to show the world Your love. Thank You for using me to build Your Kingdom. In Jesus' name, Amen.

-Written by Lynn Woolhouse

SACRED FRIENDSHIPS – Day 6

Scripture for Today:
… and when they could not get near him because of the crowd, they removed the roof above him, and when they had made an opening, they let down the bed on which the paralytic lay. And when Jesus saw their faith, he said to the paralytic, "Son, your sins are forgiven."
(Mark 2:3-5 ESV)

I Get By With a Little Help From My Friends
Doesn't it sometimes feel like you are the paralyzed man? You are stuck right where you are. There is nowhere to go, and no way to get there. It can feel like no matter how hard you try to get closer to Jesus and grow in relationship with Him, you just stay stuck. The man in this story needed his friends in order to make progress toward Jesus.

These are the types of relationships we all strive for or desperately hope to have someday. Community like this will point you back to Jesus when you are hurting - when you cannot seem to find your way closer to Him. They will tear the roof off of your situation and off the barrier that is keeping you far from Him, and help lower you right at Jesus' feet. They point you back to the only One who really knows your situation and already has victory over it.

Now, maybe you are not the paralytic in this story. Maybe you are one of the friends who tear that roof off. Remember that you get the opportunity to help someone who may be hurting or struggling get to know Jesus. You know that Jesus is worth tearing a thousand roofs off a thousand problems to show someone His grace.

Jesus wants us to have community like this. He knows that in seasons of difficulty we may need a friend who will look at us and say, "Let me remind you about that Jesus guy, you know, the One who gave His life for you." God made us to do this life in community because He knew that it is not good for us to be alone. More importantly, He made us to be close to Him. God knows that sometimes relationships are the best way for us to stay close to Him, and to find Him in the darkness.

Are you getting by with a little help from your friends? Who has God placed in your life and whose life has God placed you in to have this kind of community?

What Does God Want For You Today?

_____
_____
_____
_____
_____
_____
_____
_____

Prayer
Heavenly Father, thank You so much for building us to be in relationship with one another. Today I ask You to surround me with those who will point me toward You in the darkness. I pray that You would begin to make me that kind of friend, too, so that I can show someone else the freedom that comes from Your beautiful and courageous grace. I trust that You are already going ahead of me and preparing relationships that will speak life, love, and truth over me in every situation. In Jesus' name, Amen.

-Written by Alisyn Studeman

SACRED FRIENDSHIPS – Day 7

Scripture for Today:
Stop deceiving yourselves. If you think you are wise by this world's standards, you need to become a fool to be truly wise. (1 Corinthians 3:18 NLT)

Become Foolish
Ever wonder what it would take to become wise? To be like that old man on the mountain, who just kind of knows everything about everything? I do. I want to be wise! I want to be able to help the people in my life. When my kids have a problem, I want to help them through it. When my wife is going through hard things, I want to point her in the right direction!

So, how do we become that person? The Bible says, become foolish, or become a fool! What? I thought the whole point was to be the smartest person who has it all together? How will becoming a fool make me wiser?

If we think we know it all, will we get smarter? If we think we already know the best way to do it, will we get better at doing it? Stop thinking you know the best way, and be open to learning something new. Or just be quiet when someone tells you something you already know! That's hard, isn't it? But, if you do that, I guarantee you will become wise.

Surround yourself with people who are wiser or smarter than you! Don't just listen to anyone about a topic just because they are your friend. Sometimes our friends just give advice because they care about us - but are they wise? Should we listen to them? Look at the life of the person who you are getting advice from. Is the life they live an example of the kind of life you want? If so, listen to them! If not, find someone who has it "going on" and ask them lots of questions. Become foolish (humble yourself in order to learn from others), and you will become wise!

What Does God Want For You Today?

_____

A Prayer for Today:
Heavenly Father, help me to recognize that I can't be wise on my own! Help me to become a fool, to recognize that I don't know it all. To have wise people in my life and to put aside my own ego in order to become a wise person. In Jesus' name, Amen.

-Written by Jason Keech

SHARING YOUR HEART

**To be a Christian without prayer
is no more possible than to
be alive without breathing.**

- Martin Luther -

SHARING YOUR HEART – Day 1

Scripture for Today:
Let us then approach God's throne of grace with confidence, so that we may receive mercy and find grace to help us in our time of need. (Hebrews 4:16 NIV)

God Will Always Answer
Not to age myself too much, but back in the day before voicemail, we used to have these things called answering machines. The phone would ring a few times, and if no one picked up, the machine would kick in, "We're not available now… leave a message at the tone." The beauty of this ancient contraption was as soon as the caller began to talk, you had a choice. You could pick up the phone mid-message if you actually wanted to talk to the person on the other end of the line (you know, NOT a telemarketer). Or, you could let the machine handle the call and call the person back at a more convenient time (ahem, never).

Sometimes I think we believe God handles our prayers this way, but I have good news for you: God doesn't screen your calls. He's not up in Heaven thinking, "Dude, I just talked to you yesterday. Now what do you need? Yeah, I'll just ignore your call until I don't have anything else going on… ((click!))" NO! When we pray, God is always happily and readily available. Your prayers are not an inconvenience to God – they are a welcomed conversation starter between you and the Creator of the Universe.

You don't have to wonder if "now is a good time" to call on Him. It's always a good time. In fact, this verse says that we can come to Him in confidence. Jesus broke down that barrier between us and the Father, so He is always approachable and waiting for your call. Plus, a conversation with God offers the grace, mercy, and help you need at just the right time.

You are God's child, and He really wants to hear from you. When you call on Him today, do it with confidence. He really likes you!

What Does God Want For You Today?

_____
_____
_____
_____
_____
_____
_____
_____

A Prayer For Today:
Heavenly Father, thank You for always being there when I call. I am grateful I can turn to You at anytime for wisdom and strength. May I not shy away from any opportunities I have to encounter You today. Thank You for the grace You offer me. In Jesus' name, Amen.

-Written by Tracy Keech

SHARING YOUR HEART – Day 2

Scripture For Today:
Devote yourselves to prayer, being watchful and thankful. (Colossians 4:2 NIV)

Watchful and Thankful
Praying constantly is an important part of being a Christian. It helps us keep a healthy relationship with God throughout our day. That's what this verse is saying when it says, "Devote yourselves to prayer." In other words, pray all the time.

How do you keep a close relationship with a friend if you never talk to them? How do you tell a family member that you love them if you don't say so? It's the same thing with God and us. We can't have a close relationship with God if we never talk to Him. But we can have a close relationship with God if we include Him throughout our day.

We can have a close relationship with God by "being watchful and thankful." Every time you drive to work and you get a bunch of green lights, pray and thank God for it. Every time you find a sale at the store, pray and thank God for it. Every time your super crappy phone keeps working for another day (my phone is a piece of trash), pray and thank God for it. We need to be watchful and thankful for what God is doing in our lives! This is how we stay in touch with God.

Include Him in your seemingly average day-to-day activities. Be watchful and thankful today. Your relationship with God will be better because of it.

What Does God Want For You Today?

_____
_____
_____
_____
_____
_____
_____
_____

A Prayer For Today:
God, thank You for all that You are doing in my life. Thank You that You have given me eyes to notice You. Today, help me to be watchful and thankful for all you are doing for me. Help me to talk to You all the time to keep us close. In Jesus' name, Amen.

-Written by Braden Dykstra

SHARING YOUR HEART – Day 3

Scripture for Today:
Never stop praying. (1 Thessalonians 5:17 NLT)

Pray About Everything
When you are young, you make wishes on stars. As you get older, those wishes become dreams. As you continue to mature, those dreams become goals. And it is within these wishes, dreams, and goals that we can go through periods of doubt. That's usually when we turn to prayer.

Why must we wait for doubt to creep in before we pray? The Bible says, "Ask and it will be given, seek and you shall find, knock and the door will be opened." (Matthew 7:8) So why do we wait until we are in dire situations of doubt, fear, or disappointment to turn to our Heavenly Father who has been there the entire time? He is waiting for us to ask.

Pray about everything means exactly that! Pray about everything. Every wish, dream, and goal you have should include prayer. Not only for the wish to come true, but for the wisdom, guidance, and ability needed to accomplish that dream or goal.

Have you ever met a gymnast who didn't train? A teacher who didn't study? How about a Christian who didn't pray? How successful would they have been at their dreams had they not worked hard and focused on their source of success on a daily basis? Pray constantly, because He is there to help you prepare and open the doors for that dream to come to life, that goal to be accomplished, that wish to come true.

What Does God Want For You Today?

_____
_____
_____
_____
_____
_____
_____
_____

A Prayer For Today:
Heavenly Father, thank You for hearing my prayers. Help me to remember to pray, not just in times of need, but every day. By praying about everything in my life, I know I am inviting Your guidance, peace, and presence, through which I know all things are possible. Thank You for Your patience with me and for always being there to make my dreams come true. In Jesus' name, Amen.

-Written by Lynn Woolhouse

SHARING YOUR HEART – Day 4

Scripture for Today:
So then faith comes by hearing, and hearing by the word of God. (Romans 10:17 NKJV)

Speak The Word Of God To Your Situation
When I was fourteen, I went on a canoe trip to northern Minnesota. I was a scrawny 140 lb. kid who had to carry an 80 lb. aluminum canoe through mosquito-infested woods on mile-long portages to get from lake to lake. It was exhausting, and I became frustrated, hot, and tired, and many times wanted to just sit down and quit. To keep going, I would quote myself a Bible verse. *"I can do all things through Christ who gives me strength." (Philippians 4:13 NIV)* I said that verse out loud over and over to myself until I finally reached my destination. Quoting this verse got me through and taught me an important truth: The only thing that builds my faith and gets me through tough times is SPEAKING the Word of God.

When I have gone through a crisis, I have tried all kinds of things. I have tried to keep my chin up. I have told myself not to be angry or discouraged. I have tried to "go and do the right thing." But nothing has helped me quite like speaking God's Word to my situation.

The verse we read today says, "Faith comes by hearing and hearing by the Word of God." Or, your faith grows when you HEAR the Word of God spoken. It is like a protein shake for your soul. Just like you need protein in order to be strong physically, you need to HEAR the Word of God spoken in order to be strong spiritually. And many times, there is no one to speak the Word of God to us, so we must SPEAK IT TO OURSELVES!

You build your own faith when you speak the Word of God to your situation. What is your tough situation today? Are you facing a health issue? Find a verse on healing and speak it over and over throughout your day. I have seen many people healed through this kind of faith. Are you facing a financial struggle? Find a verse on God's provision and speak it out loud several times today. This is not a magic incantation; it is building up your faith muscles to be able to handle the struggle you face. Whatever your situation, find a verse and quote it over and over again to yourself to survive.

What Does God Want For You Today?

_____
_____
_____
_____
_____
_____
_____
_____

A Prayer For Today:
Heavenly Father, I believe that speaking Your Word to my situation will give me the strength to face it with boldness today. Your Word carries power. You spoke the world into creation. So today I will speak Your Word, knowing that it is powerful and effective and will give me faith muscles to handle what I'm going through. In Jesus' name, Amen.

-Written by Eric Dykstra

SHARING YOUR HEART – Day 5

Scripture for Today:
Always be full of joy in the Lord. I say it again - rejoice! Let everyone see that you are considerate in all you do. Remember, the Lord is coming soon. Don't worry about anything; instead, pray about everything. Tell God what you need, and thank him for all he has done. Then you will experience God's peace, which exceeds anything we can understand. His peace will guard your hearts and minds as you live in Christ Jesus. (Philippians 4:4-7 NLT)

Joy, Prayer, and Gratitude
There is a pattern that appears in this section of scripture. So often we pray, but it's not always because we want something. Sometimes, what we really want is just peace! Many times I just throw up a prayer and hope I get what I need.

The Apostle Paul in this passage reminds us of something really important. Don't just pray! First thing he says is to rejoice! Be full of joy. Think of what God has done in your life, what Christ did for you on the cross, and rejoice! Praise Him for that, be happy that you have a new life in Christ!

Then he says don't worry, pray. Don't think about how bad the situation is, don't think about how *you* need to solve the issue, just pray. Bring your need into the throne room of heaven, lay it at Christ's feet, and ask Him to help you with it!! Tell Him what you need.

And here is the last piece that is super important, don't miss this: Thank Him for all He *has* done! Christ has brought us through so much, and if we forget to thank Him for that, we miss out on the peace He has for us! Live in gratitude for all that He has done for you already, then you will have peace! Remember the pattern: joy, prayer, and gratitude.

What Does God Want For You Today?

_____
_____
_____
_____
_____
_____
_____
_____

A Prayer For Today:
Heavenly Father, I am so happy that You saved me! As I start my day, please see to all my needs. You know what I need! You know my heart and all about me, and yet You love me completely! Thank You for saving me, thank You for blessing me, thank You for all that You do. In Jesus' name, Amen.

-Written by Jason Keech

SHARING YOUR HEART – Day 6

Scripture for Today:
And how bold and free we then become in his presence, freely asking according to his will, sure that he's listening. And if we're confident that he's listening, we know that what we've asked for is as good as ours.
(1 John 5:14-15 MSG)

God Unsticks What Seems Stuck
It was one of those days. Everything was crazy, and I was rushing out the door with my kid to drop him off in time to catch the field trip bus before it left. Tie your shoes! Grab the backpack! Lock the door! Run run run. Then he said those words every parent dreads, "I still need to bring cash along for lunch." Noooooo! Not convenient. Not today. Not now. Please, no.

But, he needed it. To tack more time on to our already-rushed commute, we had to stop at the ATM. Now, I live in a fairly small town. As in, there's only one stoplight. There's not an ATM on every corner, if you know what I mean. But there *is* this one. This one, drive-up, isolated, weird, tumbleweeds-are-rolling-by-it ATM right across the street from the school. "Perfect!" I think, until I roll up to use it, punch in my PIN, get my cash, and wait for my card to come back out of it. And I wait. And then I wait some more... MY CARD WAS STUCK. Gah! Are you kidding me?!

I only freaked out a little. (I panicked.) The bus would wait. (Oh, who am I kidding? I am going to have to drive him myself!) I remained perfectly calm. ("What am I going to do now?" I wail, as I start sweating a little and tears start stinging my eyes.)

Then my son says it. "Why don't we pray?" Moment. Of. Clarity. Yes, why DON'T we pray? Why am I freaking out so much? Why isn't my first reaction to this annoying circumstance to stop and just ask God for some help? So, we prayed. Know what happened? The card came out, right on cue, as soon as I said, "Amen." No joke.

This verse says we can be bold and free in His presence. Hello… He is God. He is present all the time. This verse says God is listening all the time. Are you confident He is listening all the time? Then ask Him. Ask for the help that He can provide in an instant. Know that His will is for you to live a full and abundant life today, so when you pray for things that line up with that truth, they are as good as yours. Don't hesitate to ask Him for what you need, right now, no matter how petty or small it may seem. Trust the goodness of your Father in Heaven. He can unstick what seems stuck.

What Does God Want For You Today?

_____
_____
_____
_____
_____
_____
_____

A Prayer for Today:
Heavenly Father, I thank You that You are not only present and listening all the time, but that You actually care about even the tiniest details of my life. I believe that You have a good plan for my life, so I will trust You in prayer with all circumstances today. In Jesus' name, Amen.

-Written by Tracy Keech

SHARING YOUR HEART – Day 7

Scripture for Today:
"And I will ask the Father, and he will give you another Helper, to be with you forever, even the Spirit of truth, whom the world cannot receive, because it neither sees him nor knows him. You know him, for he dwells with you and will be in you." "But the Helper, the Holy Spirit, whom the Father will send in my name, he will teach you all things and bring to your remembrance all that I have said to you." (John 14:16-17, 26 ESV)

Direct Line to God
I used to think that if I prayed, God would only listen if He felt like it or if was high enough on His priority list that day. I thought that prayers were the only way I could connect to God, so if I wasn't praying, I wasn't connected, and therefore, God would stop paying attention. I used to wish that Jesus was still on earth so that He could be more involved in my life and I could just constantly talk to Him.

In John 16:7, Jesus actually said that it is to our advantage that He goes to heaven because then He could send the Helper. In the verse above, Jesus explains that the Helper is the Holy Spirit, that the Holy Spirit will be with us FOREVER, and that He will teach us and remind us about everything Jesus had said. SO WE HAVE A DIRECT LINE TO GOD LIVING WITH US FOREVER.

God loves us so much that He sacrificed His son Jesus so that we could spend eternity with Him. Eternity includes RIGHT NOW. We have it way better than Adam and Eve or the people that got to spend time with Jesus, because God would come and go from the Garden, Jesus would spend time alone, BUT WE HAVE THE HOLY SPIRIT 24/7!! Not to mention the Holy Spirit is what allowed Jesus to perform miracles. So the same power that raised Jesus from the dead is the same power that lives inside of us all the time!

That completely changes the way I see prayer and time with God! Having such a constant intimate connection to the Trinity means that God knows what we need and what we want before we even know to ask! Every time you eat, drink, sleep, laugh cry, pick your nose, or do absolutely anything else you can think of, God is with you and within you. The same power that healed the sick and raised the dead is the same power that lives inside of you! All Jesus did was trust that God was good and miracles happened! So trust that God is good and watch as Holy Spirit uses you to bring that same life-giving, miracle-bringing power to everyone around you!

What Does God Want For You Today?

_____
_____
_____
_____
_____
_____
_____

A Prayer for Today:
Heavenly Father, thank You for sending the Holy Spirit to live and work within me. Thank You for allowing me to have access to same resurrection power that raised Jesus from the dead. Today I pray that You would remind me about the life-giving power that You provide so I will remember to tap into it. In Jesus' name, Amen.

-Written by Alisia Sandstrom

SILENCE & SOLITUDE

We need to find God, and He cannot be found in noise and restlessness.

- Mother Theresa -

SILENCE & SOLITUDE – Day 1

Scripture for Today:
In repentance and rest is your salvation, in quietness and trust is your strength. (Isaiah 30:15 NLT)

Repent and Trust
Repent and trust can be such daunting words, but in them is the beginning of the good stuff God has for you. We are saved by grace, but when we repent (change our thinking) and choose to make new beginnings, doors of peace are opened as our choices and priorities change and resting (trusting) in our Lord begins.

How at peace did you ever feel the night of a big party? How close to Jesus did you feel after gossiping about that annoying co-worker? When we walk away from our old ways, our desires and actions begin to change. Letting go of our past (repenting), we begin to walk in the way Jesus planned, toward our destiny. With that comes the peace of a new adventure - quieting ourselves and trusting in our Creator.

When we seek God in silence and solitude, we find the rest the world cannot give us. Today, take a few moments away from every distraction to read your Bible, pray, or do something that quiets your busy mind.

When we are quiet and restful, we gain strength because it is then that we can hear the voice of God.

Despite negative finances, a rebellious child, or an aggravating boss, if you quiet yourself you will begin to embrace the peace that trusting in Jesus brings to your life.

What Does God Want For You Today?

_____
_____
_____
_____
_____
_____
_____
_____
_____

A Prayer for Today:
Heavenly Father, today I repent of the things that have kept me from embracing the peace You have for me. Give me the wisdom and clarity I need to quiet myself before You and trust You in every matter of my life. I give all my worries to You, and ask that You speak to me. Give me the ability to rest in You, knowing You will give me the strength I need. In Jesus' name, Amen.

-Written by Lynn Woolhouse

SILENCE & SOLITUDE – Day 2

Scripture for Today:
"One day soon afterwards Jesus went up on a mountain to pray, and he prayed to God all night." (Luke 6:12 NLT)

Trading Busyness for Stillness
All over scripture there are examples of times where Jesus would escape the crowds or leave His disciples to get alone in silence and solitude and pray to God. Luke 5:26 says, "But Jesus often withdrew to the wilderness for prayer." He often encouraged His disciples to do the same.

There is so much value in silence and solitude, and Jesus is our prime example of that importance. Jesus and His disciples didn't have the distractions of televisions, cell phones, Facebook, computers, etc... However they still saw the importance of disconnecting from the world to be alone in silence to connect to God. How much more are we distracted in today's world?

Is there a connection between the amount of noise in our lives and our inability to hear God? It seems that we are so hooked on productivity that the thought of being still for any period of time seems scary.

Think about the wisdom you need right now from God. Have you spent as much time in silence listening to God about your difficult situation as you have talking to others about it? Try it! What if we are waiting to hear from God in the noise while He's waiting for us in the silence?

What Does God Want For You Today?

_____
_____
_____
_____
_____
_____
_____
_____

Prayer for today
Heavenly Father, I ask that You help me get away from the distractions of the world. I ask that You would speak directly to my heart as I take time in silence. Help me get away from the distractions of the world so that I can reconnect with You. As I do so Lord, may I hear Your voice and listen to Your Word. In Jesus' name, Amen.

-Written by Mike Curtis

SILENCE & SOLITUDE – Day 3

Scripture for Today:
Jesus insisted that his disciples get back into the boat and cross to the other side of the lake, while he sent the people home. After sending them home, he went up into the hills by himself to pray. Night fell while he was there alone. (Matthew 14:22-23 NLT)

Solitude Satisfies
In this verse, Jesus had just miraculously fed more than 5,000 people from some kid's lunchbox, but then He stopped everything and sent everyone away so He could be alone. Why on earth would He stop? He seemed like He was on a roll! Not to mention that all those people came to see HIM, and He just... sent them home?

We hear all the time that God wants us to work hard and serve others, but even Jesus Himself took breaks from time to time to go be by Himself someplace quiet. In our culture today, we've forgotten the value of silence and solitude. We are surrounded by noise constantly – audible noise, yes, but also visual, emotional, and mental noise. Our thought life is so cluttered by our responsibilities and relationships that we have forgotten how to turn it all off!

That's not to say that those things aren't valuable; God wants us to have meaningful relationships, and He gives us responsibilities to serve Him and others. But Jesus is teaching us an important lesson here: solitude is just as important as serving. He knew it was important to go off by Himself to spend time with God, because God "satisfies the weary soul" (Jeremiah 31:25, ESV). Side note: being tired is okay! Even Jesus got tired – but instead of turning to caffeine or exercise or sugar, He spent time with the One who could truly refresh Him.

Find a place in your life that is free of every sort of distraction – some place where you can pray OUT LOUD. Go there to spend time alone with God. You will leave refreshed and more connected with Jesus, and better able to turn off the noise.

What Does God Want For You Today?

_____
_____
_____
_____
_____
_____
_____
_____
_____

A Prayer for Today:
Heavenly Father, I know that You can satisfy my soul like nothing else. Please help me to be refreshed when I spend time with You in silence and solitude. Give me the wisdom and the strength to turn off the noise so that I can connect with You. In Jesus' name, Amen.

-Written by Karli Phelps

SILENCE & SOLITUDE – Day 4

Scripture for Today:
Be still, and know that I am God! I will be honored by every nation. I will be honored throughout the world. (Psalm 46:10 NLT)

Turning Off the Noise
Life in the modern age is distracting. There's really no better word for it. We've become so attached to entertainment, our phones, the Internet, the hustle and bustle of work and errands and responsibilities that slowing down can be really difficult.

When we do find time or make time to slow down, we often find that the silence is scary. Our minds race, we start to think about what we're going to do after the down time. We turn on a show or occupy our brains simply so we don't have to come face-to-face with that deafening silence.

Yet God calls us to slow down, to get away from it all, turn off the noise, and simply *BE*. Why does He tell us to do this? He tells us to do this because it is one key way that we can KNOW God. Sometimes the silence will allow you to hear the voice of God, and sometimes God just wants to enjoy the silence with you.

Get intentional today by creating space for silence and solitude. It's perfectly ok to start small – start with a couple 5-minute sessions today. Separate yourself from other people, electronic devices, and activities. Get somewhere quiet and peaceful. Breathe slowly and think about Christ. Enjoy this time with your Creator. Over time this will become one of your favorite ways to connect with God because there are no barriers or distractions to hearing His voice.

What Does God Want For You Today?

_____
_____
_____
_____
_____
_____
_____
_____

A Prayer For Today:

Heavenly Father, I believe that You created me because You enjoy me. Help me to slow down today and take time to simply BE with You. Help me to enjoy this silent time with You. While I am practicing getting away from other people and the busyness of life, help me to remember that You are always with me – sometimes speaking to me, and sometimes just simply enjoying the silence with me. In Jesus' name, Amen.

-Written by Ted Snyder

SILENCE & SOLITUDE – Day 5

Scripture For Today:
...vast crowds came to hear him preach and to be healed of their diseases. But Jesus often withdrew to the wilderness for prayer. (Luke 5:16 NLT)

A Time to Attack. A Time to Withdraw.
I'm an attacker. A do-er. A mover. A talker. I'd much rather *do* than *feel. Talk* than *listen.* Sitting quietly can be hard for me. I come by this honestly. Recently my mother came to visit. Early one morning, she took her devotional book out onto the porch and said to me (very determinedly), "I'm going to sit here and read at least one page of this book." And about 30 seconds later, I heard her voice saying, "I was just calling to check on you..." She's a do-er too.

A life that is sensitive to the leading of the Holy Spirit can't always be attacking the next thing. Imagine Jesus knowing about all the people who needed Him! All the lives He could instruct and heal. And yet, He chose to withdraw *often.* He understood the importance of breaking the addiction to noise and effectiveness in the interest of feeling and hearing His Father's Spirit and instruction.

We must choose at times to withdraw, feel our feelings, and hear the "still, small voice" of the Spirit bringing peace and direction to our lives. This takes some discipline. For me, baby steps have helped. Before I attack in the morning, I withdraw with my Bible and journal. Sometimes I don't write much down, but it's an exercise in withdrawing. Exercising develops muscles. I'm developing my ability to withdraw at times when my instinct is to move.

I steal opportunities to be in silence. Times I used to

listen to music or talk on the phone, I often choose silence, like when I'm driving alone, dressing, or cooking. On the rare occasion that I'm home alone, I choose intentional silence for a time before indulging in my latest binge show.

What can you do to withdraw from the noise of people and life? To embrace periods of silence so you can talk to God and listen to the thoughts He places in your mind and heart? There's a time to attack life and live with purpose, but don't miss the times we are called to withdraw and listen.

What Does God Want For You Today?

_____
_____
_____
_____
_____
_____
_____
_____
_____

A Prayer For Today:
Heavenly Father, in the noise of life, help me to start exercising the discipline of withdrawal. As I learn to sit in the quiet, let me hear Your voice. Let me learn to be comfortable with the feelings and emotions that come up, knowing You will use them to gently shift and guide me. Thank You that I am never alone, and time spent with You is never wasted. In Jesus' name, Amen.

-Written by Kelly Dykstra

SILENCE & SOLITUDE – Day 6

Scripture for Today:
"Here's what I want you to do: Find a quiet, secluded place so you won't be tempted to role-play before God. Just be there as simply and honestly as you can manage. The focus will shift from you to God, and you will begin to sense his grace." (Matthew 6:6 MSG)

A Quiet Place with God
We live in a noisy world. It's easy to get distracted by the buzz that is always surrounding you. If it's not the hum of the fan, it's the TV, or the racing thoughts that we all can have of what's next on our to-do lists. I'm thinking about mine right now, are you?

God has given us instructions on how to take time away with Him in many places in the Bible, but we don't always take Him up on it. Going to the wilderness is an ideal place to hear and see God in nature, but it's not always practical in the day-to-day grind that we face. That is why this verse in Matthew is so important. We just need a quiet, sacred place to seek Him. It really is that easy.

I want to challenge you to do it. Set aside time just for Him in a quiet place with no agenda or to-do list. Just seek His presence. You may be surprised by what you find!

What Does God Want For You Today?

_____
_____
_____
_____
_____
_____
_____
_____

A Prayer For Today:
Heavenly Father, I come to You humbly today, knowing that You are my source. I seek You in the quiet of my heart to guide me into rest and solitude with You alone. In Jesus' name, Amen.

-Written by Christy Turner

SILENCE & SOLITUDE – Day 7

Scripture for Today:
…God called to him out of the bush, "Moses, Moses!" And he said, "Here I am." Then he said, "Do not come hear; take your sandals off your feet, for the place on which you are standing is holy ground." And he said, "I am the God of your father, the God of Abraham, the God of Isaac, and the God of Jacob." (Exodus 3:4-6 ESV)

I Dare You
Did you know that God wants to know you one-on-one? Have you ever been told that God wants you to know Him so personally that it feels like He is your best friend? It is important for you to know that God wants to know you that intimately, one-on-one, in the quiet of your heart. He is standing there waiting to meet you right where you are at; He wants a relationship with you.

If you look at the verse just before this story you see that Moses is leading a flock of sheep to the far side of the mountain, and he is all by himself when the angel of the Lord appears to him. God can and does talk to us and build relationship with us anywhere at any time, but often He waits until we are alone to appear to us. If you look at your life, are you leaving space for God? Are you leaving space for one-on-one moments with Him?

Moses' plan while going up on the mountain was not to meet with Jesus, but God saw this time as a perfect opportunity to see if Moses was open to meeting with Him. Even if you do not intentionally try to quiet your spirit to get alone with God, taking time to quiet your spirit will leave space for Jesus to show up in so many ways. He is just waiting for the moment when your heart is prepared and ready to receive what He already has for you.

We all have different ways of getting quiet and leaning into quiet time with Jesus. The best thing you can do is discover the way that quiets your spirit. Maybe you go for a walk in the woods. Maybe you need to take a drive. Maybe you need to lay in bed and pull the covers over your head. Or maybe you need to journal your heart out to Him. Whatever it is, Jesus is already waiting to meet you. He knows where you are because He is already with you. He is just waiting for you to get quiet so that when He appears to you, you'll actually recognize Him. What do you think your pathway to Jesus looks like? I dare you to go get quiet there and invite God to show up. You might be surprised at His response.

What Does God Want For You Today?

_____
_____
_____
_____
_____
_____
_____
_____

A Prayer For Today:
Heavenly Father, I pray that You would give me opportunities to quiet my spirit and my life. Please show up as I get alone and away from the hustle and bustle of the world. I invite You, the God of relationship, to meet with me one-on-one so that I can hear all that You have to share with me. Pursue me relentlessly so that I can know You better and walk in the good plans You have for my life. In Jesus' name, Amen.

-Written by Alisyn Studeman

SENT ONES

We're on a mission from God.

- The Blues Brothers -

SENT ONES – Day 1

Scripture for Today:
But my life is worth nothing to me unless I use it for finishing the work assigned me by the Lord Jesus - the work of telling others the Good News about the wonderful grace of God. (Acts 20:24 NLT)

Our Greatest Assignment
There are all kinds of great things we can do in life. Cure diseases, fight poverty, teach people to read and write, help the homeless, seek to end racism, feed starving children, fight sex trafficking. There are so many great causes in the world that need to be addressed, but there is one cause greater than all the other causes. There is one mission greater than all the other missions. There is one task greater than all the other tasks: "Telling others the good news about the wonderful grace of God."

Grace is God's unearned, undeserved, never-ending FAVOR toward all people on earth. God sent His son Jesus to die in our place and take the punishment for our sins so that we would never face the wrath of God. According to the scriptures, Jesus took our beating for sin so you and I could be be blessed, approved, and favored by God. It is the BEST NEWS ever. Jesus did the work so you and I could be friends with God!

Once we know this truth for ourselves, we have the greatest task ever: to tell other people about the wonderful grace of God! This is our number one job as believers in Jesus. We share grace with others.

So, who will you tell this week? Who will you talk to about the grace of God? What person in your life needs to know that God is for them and not against them? Go and tell them! They need grace today!

What Does God Want For You Today?

_____
_____
_____
_____
_____
_____
_____
_____
_____

A Prayer For Today:
Heavenly Father, I believe that speaking about Your wonderful grace is my greatest task as a follower of Christ. Today give me the courage, love, and boldness to speak up to someone else about how much You love them! Help me not be silent, but instead be vocal that You are not mad at people, but that You are for us because Jesus died for us. May I speak up today! In Jesus' name, Amen.

-Written by Eric Dykstra

SENT ONES – Day 2

Scripture for Today:
"You did not choose Me but I chose you, and appointed you that you would go and bear fruit, and that your fruit would remain, so that whatever you ask of the Father in My name He may give to you. (John 15:16 NIV)

He Chose You
Notice the word choice, "You did not choose me, but I chose you." Why does He say, "You did not choose me?" We do choose to follow Jesus. He does not drag us around kicking and screaming. He does not handcuff us to His side. We aren't actively looking for ways to escape Him once we've found Him. We do chose Him.

Let's flip it. What if instead Jesus said, "I did not choose you; you chose Me?" What would be the point of saying it that way? It might mean, "Look, I have no ties to you. You came to Me. Don't come crying to me when things fall apart because this was your choice. I lay no claim on anything in your life."

But thankfully, Jesus said the opposite. "You did not choose Me, but I chose you." I believe that He is saying, "Your presence is My doing, and so I take full responsibility. I know you agreed to join Me in this work, but deep in your head, you know it was I who laid claim on you and so My honor, not yours, is at stake in this work."

If that is what Jesus means, then the reason He said, "You did not choose me, but I chose you" was to encourage us that He would help us. If His honor is at stake in our success because He chose us for the work, then we can be sure He will exhaust all His power to make us fruitful in all we do. Plus He will make it last for all eternity!

What Does God Want For You Today?

_____
_____
_____
_____
_____
_____
_____
_____

A Prayer for Today:
Heavenly Father, thank You for Your goodness. Thank You for laying claim on me as Your chosen one. Thank You for allowing me to do the work, while You do the heavy lifting. Thank You for assigning me a task, but that the effort is all Yours. Thank You for calling me to something so much greater than mere existence. In Jesus' name, Amen.

-Written by Maria Sandstrom

SENT ONES – Day 3

Scripture for Today:
Come close to God, and God will come close to you. Wash your hands, you sinners; purify your hearts, for your loyalty is divided between God and the world. (James 4:8 NLT)

Hands and Feet
Life is busy. Sometimes we think we'll have so much more time once the kids are older or grown and gone. I have found that once the kids grow up, there are other things that come and fill up our time. Just as "things" fill up your time, don't forget take time to fill up with God every day.

Taking time to read God's Word or spend time with Him is like washing your hands spiritually. When we wash our hands physically, it's usually to prepare for doing something important, like serving meals to people who are hungry. When our own hands are clean, we are able to be the hands and feet of Jesus to the rest of the world. You will be effective with the mission God has for you when you start out by spending time with Him.

Come close to God today and He will come close to you. He will help you be focused on the purpose you were created for. How are you going to make time for Him every day?

Wash yourself in the Word today. We have something important to do! We get to go out and be Jesus to our world!

What Does God Want For You Today?

_____
_____
_____
_____
_____
_____
_____
_____

A Prayer for Today:
Heavenly Father, thank You for giving me a purpose and mission. I want to start being Your hands and feet by connecting with You first. I am ready to do Your work today. In Jesus' name, Amen.

-Written by Amy Kingore

SENT ONES – Day 4

Scripture For Today:
God saved you by his grace when you believed. And you can't take credit for this; it is a gift from God. Salvation is not a reward for the good things we have done, so none of us can boast about it. For we are God's masterpiece. He has created us anew in Christ Jesus, so we can do the good things he planned for us long ago.
(Ephesians 2:8-10 NLT)

So-That
If it's true that we have a Creator God who is actively working in our world and lives, not one single day of your life is without purpose. There's always a so-that. This set of verses tells us that our salvation from sin and death and eternity without God extends beyond our own benefit. We are given this gift and our unique design SO THAT we can do good in the world.

First the writer reminds us that God's grace cannot be earned. *So that* you don't get all hoity-toity and try to brag about how spiritual and holy you made yourself.

Then He mentions the whole God-created-you-from-His-brilliant-imagination thing *so that* you don't get the idea that you're so clever to have gotten yourself to where you are at this point in your life.

And then He brings up the part about how we're created completely new IN Jesus *so that* we can DO THE GOOD THINGS He dreamed up ages ago, before He even made you, you little masterpiece, you.

A masterpiece has a purpose. It speaks of the brilliance of the Master. I want to remind you today that you have been created. New. In Jesus. To speak of the brilliance of your Master Creator and DO the things you were gifted and created to do. Don't just sit on a shelf and feel important on your own. Live with His purposes in mind today - SO THAT other people can find out that God loves them and created them with purpose too.

What Does God Want For You Today?

_____
_____
_____
_____
_____
_____
_____
_____

A Prayer For Today:
Heavenly Father, let me never forget that I have been created and saved from a purposeless, hopeless life SO THAT others can experience the same. Thank You for giving me purpose. Let me show my world Your brilliance and grace. Help me see and use opportunities to do good and point people to You. In Jesus' name, Amen.

-Written by Kelly Dykstra

SENT ONES – Day 5

Scripture for Today:
But when they did not find them, they dragged Jason and some of the brethren to the rulers of the city, crying out, "These who have turned the world upside down have come here too!" (Acts 17:6 NKJV)

Upside Down
This passage of scripture intrigues me. "These who have turned the world upside down..." Makes me think, why were they so impactful? I'm quite sure that these guys didn't have the goal of being world-changers. That's what is so interesting to me.

When I started following Christ, I was just a regular guy. I didn't have a long-term goal of making the world a better place or trying to let people know about God or any goal for that matter.

You see, just like you, I'm just a normal person. I'm trying to make ends meet, have a roof over my head, raise my kids, and love my wife and family well. That's where the good news comes in. That's where Jesus enters the picture.

There is nothing special about the men and women in the Bible. But what's cool is that when Christ comes into your life, something changes. Things look different, and you become different. Your goal may not be to change the world, but the very nature of having the Spirit of God in you changes everything in your environment!

What if you leaned into that strength and started to follow what God wants to do with you! I bet your world would change! God will use you to change the world around you. Will you let Him?

What Does God Want For You Today?

_____
_____
_____
_____
_____
_____
_____
_____
_____

A Prayer for Today:
Heavenly Father, sometimes I think the pressure is all on me to be a world-changer. Help me to remember that I am not responsible for that - You are. Let me embrace what You want to do through me. I am open to whatever You want to do with me. Let's turn the world upside-down! In Jesus' name, Amen.

-Written by Jason Keech

SENT ONES – Day 6

Scripture for Today:
For we are [God's] workmanship, created in Christ Jesus for good words, which God prepared beforehand, that we should walk in them. (Ephesians 2:10 ESV)

Mission: [Im]Possible
This verse feels like the beginning of one of those great speeches. You know, the ones where it's obvious that we are going to be called to go do something super amazing, life-changing, and ultimately exciting and dangerous. However, this speech came thousands of years before, "I have a dream..." or, "We hold these truths to be self-evident..."

This speech is the speech that will lay the foundation for all the rest. Paul is reminding the Ephesians that our works are not what put us in favor with God. No, Paul is trying to help the Ephesians (and us) understand that it is God that has prepared good works for us, and that He created us for those good works. It is His grace that gives us the motivation to even want to do those works.

Still, "the works" - good, bad or otherwise - are not the focus. It is not even the fact that we "should walk in them." Paul's speech is one that pumps adrenaline through your veins, gets your heart racing, your palms sweaty, and your feet ready to run as fast and as far as they can take you.

What Paul is really hoping we will understand is that God made us each with a Mission: Possible. Now, that's not to say it will seem possible in the moment. In fact, it will look like Mission: Impossible from every angle except God's. Upon completion, this mission will give all the glory to God, because there was no way to do it without Him.

That is the beauty of this mission. It is only possible because God is the One who laid it out for you and He laid it out for ONLY you. He isn't going to just give this to anyone else. He planned it, designed it, and uniquely set it up just for you and Him to do together. His mission for us, when finished, will feel like the most amazing thing we have ever done because we were made to fulfill it. It was made because Jesus believed that only we alone could fulfill such a mission.

Now I have a big question for you. What's your Mission: [Im]Possible? Will you choose to accept it?

What Does God Want For You Today?
_____
_____
_____
_____
_____
_____
_____
_____

A Prayer for Today:
Heavenly Father, I pray that today You would begin to stir in me the mission that You planned for me. Give me the courage and strength to chase after it. Though it may seem impossible, I ask that You will give me the confidence to keep walking through it. I trust You to work in the impossible places. Thank You for believing in me enough to entrust to me such a valuable and perfectly designed mission. In Jesus' name, Amen.

-Written by Alisyn Studeman

SENT ONES – Day 7

Scripture for Today:
Therefore, go and make disciples of all the nations, baptizing them in the name of the Father and the Son and the Holy Spirit. Teach these new disciples to obey all the commands I have given you. And be sure of this: I am with you always, even to the end of the age. (Matthew 28:19-20 NLT)

Well, That Seems Daunting

Whoa. This seems like a really big job. Go and make disciples of ALL the nations? BAPTIZE everyone? What if I find them in the desert? Teach them to OBEY all the commands? ALL of them, Jesus? Are you sure? I don't even have a 100% success rate on getting my teenagers to do the dishes without being told!

I'm pretty sure Jesus wraps up the Great Commission by promising He'll always be with us because He knows how daunting this mission can seem. It seems like a lot of pressure to, you know, be the ones solely responsible for changing the entire world. The thing is: we aren't.

Let's go back to Genesis. When God decided to make people, He chose to make us in His image. That's pretty good news if you ask me, because doing anything in my own strength sounds like a downer. But God says I don't need to rely on my own efforts to accomplish His purpose. He created me in His image, and He also put His Spirit inside me, giving me the power to accomplish what only He can do. My only role is to remain in step with Him. If I continue to believe He is doing all the work, I can keep moving forward in joy. It's a drag to do a job all by yourself, but it's really fun to join God where He is already working!

If you find yourself in a disciple-making, Kingdom-building, faith-sharing opportunity today, remember that Jesus is WITH you, and He is the One doing all the work. The pressure's off. Don't sweat it. God's got you, and He's giving you the words, wisdom, and power you need for today.

What Does God Want For You Today?

_____
_____
_____
_____
_____
_____
_____
_____

A Prayer for Today:
Heavenly Father, I am grateful that I get to be on Your team! Let me not become overwhelmed by the mission to reach this world with Your grace. It is not my job to carry burdens, but to listen to Your voice about when and where to move next. I am excited to be able to join You at work today. I can't wait to see what we get to do next! In Jesus' name, Amen.

-Written by Tracy Keech

SENT ONES – Day 8

Scripture for Today:
But how can they call on him to save them unless they believe in him? And how can they believe in him if they have never heard about him? And how can they hear about him unless someone tells them? And how will anyone go and tell them without being sent? That is why the Scriptures say, "How beautiful are the feet of messengers who bring good news!" (Romans 10:14-15)

Calling All Messengers
We've been given a calling to share the Good News of Jesus. We've been forgiven, and now that we know His truths, we want to shout it from the mountaintops! It's the fire of being a new believer or reborn in Christ. It is point blank the best feeling in the world!

Sometimes being a messenger is more that just telling a person about the goodness of Jesus. It's about showing them just how good He is. "Jesus loves you! He has a great life planned for you! You are royalty! You mean more to Him than you can even imagine." We can tell people these things all day long, but it means so much more when it's accompanied with action.

At The Crossing Church, I am known as the "Haiti Lady". I have been blessed to be the team leader for several mission trips to the orphanage that our church supports in Port Au Prince. Every time we travel to this decimated but beautiful country, we come with tasks in mind. Build a new roof, put in a septic, pour a foundation… Why? Because we can tell these kiddos with our words that Jesus loves them, but when they can physically SEE Jesus loving them THROUGH US, it grows their faith.

God wants to save the rest of the world just as He has saved you. What if you did something tangible to show someone else God loves them today? Make a donation, volunteer your time, or do something kind. Let your message be accompanied by action, and see what happens!

What Does God Want For You Today?

_____
_____
_____
_____
_____
_____
_____
_____

A Prayer For Today:
Heavenly Father, thank You for the new life You gave me! I am grateful that I get to be Your child. Will You help me today to see all the ways You want to work in the lives of the people around me? Please help me share Your love with actions, not just with words. In Jesus' name, Amen.

-Written by Christy Turner

The Crossing Church (freegrace.tv) is based in Elk River, Minnesota, with campuses in surrounding towns. It is known widely for its unique approach to reaching those who feel the need for God's grace the most. The grace message and its accompanying Holy Spirit power is continually transforming the people of The Crossing.

The Crossing College (TheCrossingCollege.com) offers two programs - a Diploma in Biblical Studies and an Associates in Church Leadership and Ministry - that were designed to equip members of the Body of Christ for living out their calling. The programs are affordable, able to be completed within 1-2 years, and fit within a normal life schedule.

Crossing Creative (CrossingCreative.com) leads The Crossing Church in worship and publishes original worship music. *Grace is Life* is their debut album, combining intentional, grace-centric lyrics with their signature rock & roll-style of worship. Their second album is called *Found My Worth*. Both are available on iTunes and Amazon.

Eric Dykstra is a former freaked-out Christian overachiever who is now resting in the grace of God found in the New Covenant. He and his wife Kelly founded The Crossing, a multi-site church north of Minneapolis. Eric's passions include seeing broken people far from God come to know the amazing grace of Jesus, fishing for smallmouth bass, and traveling with his family. *Grace on Tap* is Eric's first book, released in 2013. He also co-authored *Unhooked & Untangled: A Guide to Finding Freedom from your Vices, Addictions, and Bad Habits*. Both books are available on Amazon and Amazon Kindle.

Kelly Dykstra loves helping people discover that a life of faith is simpler than you'd think. Raised in Alabama, Kelly is a southern girl at heart. She finds great delight in olives, Mexican food, traveling, high heels, and going out to eat with Eric and her kiddos, Braden, Holland & Aidan. *The People Mover* is Kelly's first book, released in 2014. Available on Amazon and Amazon Kindle.

You can find Eric & Kelly's ministry and sermons on freegrace.tv.